MONET
BY

La Japonaise, 1875–6, Museum of Fine Arts, Boston

MONET
BY

ARTISTS BY THEMSELVES
EDITED BY RACHEL BARNES

ALFRED A. KNOPF
NEW YORK
1990

This is a Borzoi Book
Published by Alfred A. Knopf, Inc.

Introduction Text Copyright © 1990 by Rachel Barnes

All rights reserved under International and Pan-American Copyright Conventions.
Published in the United States by Alfred A. Knopf, Inc.
Distributed by Random House, Inc., New York.

Originally published in Great Britain by
Webb & Bower (Publishers) Limited, Exeter, Devon

Series devised by Nicky Bird

Designed by Vic Giolitto

Library of Congress Cataloging-in-Publication Data
Barnes, Rachel.
    Artists by themselves. Monet/Rachel Barnes. — 1st American ed.
      p. cm.
    "Originally published in Great Britain by Webb & Bower
(Publishers) Limited, Exeter"—T.p. verso.
    ISBN 0–394–58906–8 : $16.95
    1. Monet, Claude. 1840–1926 — Sources. 2. Painting — Themes.
motives. I. Title.
ND553.M7B37 1990
759.4 — dc20   90–52732
                                      CIP

Manufactured in Italy
First American Edition

CONTENTS

Introduction   6

Monet by Monet   18

Chronology   78

Acknowledgements   80

INTRODUCTION

'I would like to paint as the bird sings.' Whenever Claude Monet talked or wrote about his art it was his role as an interpreter of nature and the natural world that he emphasized. His response to everything he saw about him, and its subsequent translation into paint, were amongst the most direct and heartfelt in the history of Western art; it was this joyful and spontaneous response to the visual world that the painter Paul Cézanne was referring to when he exclaimed 'Monet is only an eye, but my God, what an eye!'

Claude Monet was the primary inspiration of the Impressionist movement. Indeed his painting 'Impression, Sunrise' of 1872, with its dappled, pointillist technique and obsession with light, atmosphere and colour, gave the movement its name: on seeing the painting at the group's first exhibition in 1874, the critic Louis Leroy recoiled in horror, feeling it to be not a painting at all but, as its title might suggest, merely an impression.

Over a century later the wheel has come full circle, and a movement that was initially rebellious and challenging to traditional artistic values has become completely accepted. Yet, looking at the work of Monet it is impossible not to be struck by the breathtaking freshness and vitality evident in his response to nature – few painters' perceptions of natural beauty have been so acute that the viewer's own appreciation of nature is enhanced. Monet wanted to convey that sense of almost child-like wonder and was keenly aware of his own ability – his genius – which enabled him to do this. He once said to his friend Lilla Cabot Perry that 'he wished he had been born blind and then had suddenly gained his sight so that he could

Claude Monet in his garden, 1926, Droits résérves; Document Archives
Durand-Ruel

have begun to paint . . . without knowing what the objects were that
he saw before him'.

Monet was born in Paris in 1840, but his family moved to Le
Havre on the coast when he was only five. Later he felt that being
brought up close to the sea – which was always to stimulate and
excite him – was crucial to the development of his visual responses,
particularly to the light and atmosphere which so governed his
inspiration.

Monet's father ran a comparatively prosperous wholesale grocery business in Le Havre. Determined from early adolescence to paint, · Monet finally persuaded his father to let him go to Paris to study at the studio of Charles Gleyre. Gleyre's tuition, however, turned out to be rather less important than Monet's meeting with Renoir, which marked the beginning of a lifelong friendship. Together, in the summer of 1869, they went down to La Grenouillère on the Seine, where they painted all the everyday, outdoor scenes that caught their attention. It was at this time that the foundations of Impressionism were laid: the insistence on the revolutionary practice of painting *en plein air*; the evolution of the pointillist technique; the interest in ordinary *quotidien* subject matter, as Baudelaire expressed it; and, perhaps above all (certainly in Monet's case), the preoccupation with light, weather and atmosphere. 'It was as if a veil was torn from my eyes and I understood what painting could be,' Monet was to write later of this crucial period.

It was this obsession – it hardly amounted to less – which led Monet to experiment continually, often braving appalling weather conditions in his zeal to record light and atmosphere as faithfully as possible. On one excursion to the coast at Etretat he was almost engulfed by a huge wave as a result of misreading the tide tables; in the winter months he wrote to his family describing how his beard had grown icicles during one particularly grim session of *plein air* painting, where he had himself fastened to the ice, with a hot water bottle to keep his hand warm enough to paint. Something of his courage, dedication and determination is reflected in these rather farcical stories.

During the Franco-Prussion War in 1870 Monet and Pissarro both escaped the horrors of Paris for London, where Monet was to paint the first of his foggy, atmospheric series of the Thames (see p

The Artist's Garden at Vétheuil, 1880, National Gallery of Art, Washington DC;
Ailsa Mellon Bruce Collection

Antibes, 1888, Toledo Museum of Art, Ohio

29). Later, when he returned there in 1899, he told René Gimpel, 'I like London only in the winter; without the fog, London would not be a beautiful city. It is the fog which gives it its marvellous breadth. Its regular, massive blocks became grandiose in this mysterious cloak.'

On returning to France in 1871, Monet moved out of Paris to Argenteuil. By this time he had met his future wife, Camille Doncieux, who was to remain with him until her premature death from tuberculosis in 1879. Although their relationship was at times turbulent, theirs was a strong bond and Monet suffered deep depression for some time after her death. He immortalized her, frequently accompanied by their eldest son Jean, in a number of paintings, and often in the gardens which so inspired his love of colour.

This period in Argenteuil, before the first Impressionist show, was the time when Monet painted his most essentially Impressionist works: the river scenes, often executed from his studio boat; the countryside around the village, painted in different seasons and weather conditions – but also the modern, industrial landscapes with factory chimneys in the background. Here Monet was often visited by Sisley, Renoir and Manet, and together during the course of the 1870s the group consolidated their aims and technique.

By 1878, however, Monet felt so disillusioned by the spectacular failure of the first three group exhibitions that he no longer sought the proximity of the capital, and he decided to move further down the river to Vétheuil, where he and his family set up house with his former patron Ernest Hoschedé and his wife Alice. Only a year later Camille died and Hoschedé left his family, having suffered a mental collapse as a result of financial disaster. This left Alice Hoschedé and Monet in charge of their eight children, and they were to remain together, marrying after Hoschedé's death in 1892, until Alice's own death in 1911.

Monet did a good deal of travelling in the 1880s, often to the coastal resorts of Normandy and Etretat, and always in search of unusual, often dramatic weather. It was at this time that Japanese prints, which had been of interest to experimental artists since their importation into Paris in the 1850s, began to play an increasingly important part in his work. The stark, bold compositions, the unusual viewpoint and the juxtaposition of strong colour all influenced the development of Monet's approach to landscape.

From 1890, after his move to Giverny, Monet travelled much

The Tuilleries, 1876, Musée Marmottan, Paris

less, concentrating more on his new interest: series of pictures showing the same subject in different light. He began by painting a couple of haystacks grouped in a field near his house. Although superficially an uninspiring theme, by choosing something so simple Monet was able to explore his concept that every object becomes completely transformed when seen at different times of the day or in different seasons. In 1890 he wrote:

> For me, a landscape does not exist in its own right, since its appearance changes at every moment; but the surrounding atmosphere brings it to life – the light and the air which vary

continually. For me, it is only the surrounding atmosphere which gives subjects their true value.

The following year he repeated the same experiment with 'The Poplars' and then, in 1894, transferred his idea to architecture, painting Rouen Cathedral at hourly intervals throughout the day and evening. He insisted it was essential that the series be viewed together in order for his idea to be understood; sadly, today very few of them are hung in the same room.

The final expression of this fascination with thematic painting was the work of his last years, the 'Nympheas', his decorative paintings and friezes of water-lilies which he painted in his garden

Gladioli, 1876, Founders Society, Detroit Institute of Arts

Poppy Field in a Hollow near Giverny, 1885, Museum of Fine Arts, Boston

at Giverny. The garden, with its photogenic pond and Japanese bridge, was not specifically designed to be painted, but Monet soon realized its potential. Practically, it was of great benefit in his later years as he became increasingly immobile and infirm – he was working on the last of his water-lily paintings in the 1920s as an old man. Despite the onset of blindness caused by cataracts his art never stopped developing, and his last works are almost pure colour abstractions, bearing increasingly less relation to any figurative concept.

In many of the excerpts from Monet's letters which are

reproduced in this book, the reader is made aware of the artist's trials and tribulations before the forces of nature, his frustration and depression when his work was going badly or was held up by impossible weather conditions, and his excitement and inspiration when some dramatic natural phenomenom caught his artist's eye. Like most painters of originality and genius, Monet was prone to fits of black despondency when his work was not going well. In 1912 he wrote to Durand-Ruel, the dealer, in bitter disappointment when the exhibition of his paintings of Venice opened:

Sheltered Path, 1873, Philadelphia Museum of Art: Given by Mr and Mrs Hughes Norment in honour of William H. Donner

Monet walking in his garden, 1926, Droits résérves; Document Archives Durand-Ruel

... More than ever today, I realize how artificial is the undeserved fame I have won. I keep hoping to do better, but age and sorrow have drained my strength. I know beforehand that you'll say my pictures are perfect. I know that when shown they will be much admired but I don't care because I know they are bad. I'm certain of it. Thank you for your comforting words, your friendship and all the trouble you have taken.

These sad and despondent words show that even popular and critical acclaim did not always give Monet self confidence, even after the early years of rejection and hardship were long past. Fortunately, such despair alternated with more optimistic moods. He thought and spoke continually about his art: the well known story of his viewing with fascination the changing skin tone of his wife Camille on her death bed is evidence of his being an artist above all else. He loved his wife, despite their frequently disturbed relationship, and deeply mourned her death, yet he wrote with guilt and honesty that, even at this traumatic moment, he could not help observing and recording as a painter.

'I perhaps owe having become a painter to flowers,' Monet wrote in 1924, towards the end of his life, when his water-lilies had completely filled his artistic vision. His art began with flowers, and it ended with flowers. In the pages that follow, crucial extracts from Monet's letters and writings are quoted next to the relevant painting, providing an insight into the artist's genius and purpose, and revealing his overwhelming fascination with the metamorphoses of nature.

Self Portrait
1878

Private Collection

Paint as you see nature yourself. If you don't see nature right with an individual feeling, you will never be a painter, and all the teaching cannot make you one. A painter must work out his own problem in his art, as everyone must work out his own problem in life.

Cited in D. Wildenstein
Monet, Biography and Catalogue Raisonné, 1974

[19]

Le Havre at Low Tide
1865

Kimbell Art Museum, Fort Worth, Texas

Really, you never seem to lose interest in me. I am honoured indeed; however, it's Boudin who concerns us here. On this matter, concerning my relationship with the 'King of skies', I think I've already told you that I consider Boudin as my Master.

You are quite right, I did meet Boudin, my senior, I believe, by about fifteen years, in Le Havre, while I was struggling to earn a reputation as a caricaturist. It's true that I was fifteen or so at the time. I was known throughout the town of Le Havre. I charged between 10 and 20 francs for my portraits and signed them Oscar, my second name. I often exhibited them with Boudin, whose painting I didn't appreciate at first, influenced as I was by academic theories. Troyon and Millet also frequented the gallery shop. One day Boudin said to me: 'You're talented, you should drop this kind of work which you'll tire of sooner or later. Your sketches are excellent, you're not going to leave it at that. Do what I do, learn to draw well and appreciate the sea, light, the blue sky.' I took his advice and together we went on long outings during which I painted constantly from nature. That was how I came to understand nature and learnt to love it passionately and how I became interested in the high-keyed painting of Boudin. It should be remembered that he had received some training from a master, Jongkind, whose work (his watercolours in particular) lies with Corot's at the origin of what has been called Impressionism. I've said it before and can only repeat that I owe everything to Boudin and I attribute my success to him. I came to be fascinated by his studies, the products of what I call instantaneity.

Letter to Gustav Geffroy, Giverny, 1920

Camille

1866

Kunsthalle, Bremen

The portrait bought for the Bremen Museum was executed in Paris in 1866 and exhibited at the Salon of that year. Madame Monet, my first wife, did indeed model for it and while I hadn't set out specifically to do a portrait, but merely a Parisian lady of the period, the resemblance is striking.

The painting was known generally as the 'Woman with a Green Dress'. I sold it in 1868 to Arsène Houssaye, the former director of the Comédie Française who was at that time attached to the Beaux-Arts as an inspector of national museums.

He bought it for himself, intending to bequeath it later on to the Musée du Luxembourg (for at that time everyone or almost everyone was against me). But he died before public opinion changed and his son, Henri Houssaye, a member of the Académie Française, was quick to dispose of the painting for a derisory sum of money. Things changed later on and the same picture was much admired.

That is all I can tell you, but I must also say how glad I am to know it is in your museum and that I am very flattered.

Letter to Gustav Pauli, Giverny, May 1906

Bathers at La Grenouillère
1869

National Gallery, London

Alas! Once again I will not appear there [at the Salon], since I have nothing finished. I do have a dream, a tableau of the bathers at La Grenouillère, for which I've done some bad pôchades. Renoir, who has just spent a couple of months here, has already attempted it . . .

Cited in D. Wildenstein
Monet, Biography and Catalogue Raisonné, 1974

Regatta at Argenteuil
1872

Musée d'Orsay, Paris

It is indeed frighteningly difficult to do something that is complete in every respect, and I believe there are very few people who are satisfied with approximations. So, my friend, I want to struggle, scrape out, start again, because one can do what one sees and understands, and it seems to me when I am looking at nature that I am going to do everything, write it all down, but then just try to accomplish it . . . when you're there before the canvas . . .

All of which proves that we must think of nothing else. It is through observation and reflection that one finds.

Letter to Fréderic Bazille, 1864

The Thames Below Westminster
1872

National Gallery, London

In the early hours of this morning there was an extraordinary completely yellow fog; I did an impression of it which I don't think is bad; otherwise it's still fine, but very variable; so I had to start lots of canvases of Waterloo Bridge and the Houses of Parliament; I also resumed work on several paintings done on the first trip, the least good ones. I'm mostly working here for the time being, and don't go to the hospital until 4 in the afternoon. Unfortunately the fog doesn't seem to want to lift and I fear the morning will be wasted.

Letter to Alice Monet, London, February 1900

Rough Sea, Etretat
1873

Musée d'Orsay, Paris

... I've done an excellent day's work today, I'm very happy and what's more the weather is superb even though a little cold. I intend to do a large painting of the cliff at Etretat, although it is terribly bold of me to do so after Courbet has painted it so admirably, but I will try to do it in a different way ...

Letter to Alice Hoschedé, Etretat, 1873

Gare St Lazarre
1877

National Gallery, London

The general lack of understanding gave Monet an irresistible desire to do a painting still more foggy.

One day he said to Renoir triumphantly:

'I've got it! The Gare Saint-Lazarre! I'll show it just as the trains are starting, with smoke from the engines so thick you can hardly see a thing. It's a fascinating sight, a regular dreamworld.'

He did not, of course, intend to paint it from memory. He would paint it *in situ* so as to capture the play of sunlight on the steam rising from the locomotives.

'I'll get them to delay the train for Rouen half an hour. The light will be better then.'

'You're mad,' said Renoir.

Jean Renoir
Renoir, My Father, 1962

Camille on her Death Bed
1879

Musée d'Orsay, Paris

My poor wife gave up the struggle this morning at 10.30 after the most ghastly suffering. I am in a state of terrible distress finding myself alone with my poor children.

Letter to Georges de Bellio, Vétheuil, 1879

It is my day-long obsession, joy and torment. To such an extent indeed that one day, finding myself at the death-bed of a woman who had been and was still very dear to me, I caught myself, with my eyes focused on her tragic temples, in the act of automatically searching for the succession, the arrangement of coloured gradations that death was imposing on her motionless face. Blue, yellow, grey tones, who knows what else? That was the point I had reached. Nothing is more natural than the urge to record one last image of a person departing this life. But even before I had the idea of recording those features to which I was so profoundly attached, my organism was already reacting to the colour sensations, and, in spite of myself, I was being involved by my reflexes in an unconscious process in which I was resuming the course of my daily life.

Conversation reported by Georges Clemenceau

The Banks of the Seine, near Vétheuil

1880

National Gallery of Art, Washington DC

For me, a landscape does not exist in its own right, since its appearance changes at every moment; but its surroundings bring it to life – the air and the light, which vary continually ... For me, it is only the surrounding atmosphere which gives objects their real value.

Cited in D. Wildenstein
Monet, Biography and Catalogue Raisonné, 1974

Low Tide at Pourville
1882

Cleveland Museum of Art
Gift of Mrs Henry White Cannon

I am completely discouraged. After several days of beautiful weather, the rain has started again, and once more I have to put aside the things I have begun. I am going crazy and unfortunately it's my poor canvases that I take it out on. A large still-life of flowers that I just finished I have destroyed along with three or four canvases that I have not only scraped out but slashed ... I see the future too black. Doubt has taken possession of me, I feel lost, I'll no longer be able to do anything.

Letter to Durand-Ruel, September 1882

Beach at Dieppe
1882

... I've had a very tiring day, I've been all over the countryside, along all the paths below and above the cliffs. I've seen some lovely things and I was helped by superb sunshine, but even so I'm afraid that I might not be able to work as well as I did at Fécamp. It has a lot to do with my set up, and it's too close to the centre of town. Anyway, tomorrow I'll do some more exploring and the day after I'll set to work and depending on how I do, I'll see whether I should stay here, or go back to Fécamp or Yport. The truth is, I don't feel at ease and I am bored. Don't fail to send me your news regularly and make sure you tell Jean to write. You didn't tell me whether the children, big and small, are better. Hug them all warmly for me, best wishes to Marthe. For you my warmest thoughts.

Letter to Alice Hoschedé, Dieppe, February 1882

Bordighera
1884

Art Institute of Chicago

I've been working non-stop today right up to 6 o'clock this evening, and took only an hour off for lunch, but I worked well and am very satisfied with what I've done today; what a lot of daubs I did in the beginning, but now I've caught this magical landscape and it's the enchantment of it that I'm so keen to render. Of course lots of people will protest that it's quite unreal and that I'm out of my mind, but that's just too bad, anyway that's what they say when I paint our part of the world.

They may excite a bit the enemies of blue and pink, because it is exactly the sparkle, this enchanted light that I am determined to render, and those who haven't seen this country, or have seen it wrongly, will protest, I'm sure, the lack of resemblance, although I am well below the tone: everything is iridescent.

Letters to Alice Hoschedé, Bordighera, 1884

Etretat
1885

After another rainy morning I was glad to find the weather slightly improved: despite a high wind blowing and a rough sea, or rather, because of it, I hoped for a fruitful session at the Manneporte; however an accident befell me. Don't alarm yourself now, I am safe and sound since I'm writing to you, although you nearly had no news and I would never have seen you again. I was hard at work beneath the cliff, well sheltered from the wind, in the spot which you visited with me; convinced that the tide was drawing out I took no notice of the waves which came and fell a few feet away from me. In short, absorbed as I was, I didn't see a huge wave coming; it threw me against the cliff and I was tossed about in its wake along with all my materials! My immediate thought was that I was done for, as the water dragged me down, but in the end I managed to clamber out on all fours, but Lord, what a state I was in! My boots, my thick stockings and my coat were soaked through; the palette which I had kept a grip on had been knocked over my face and my beard was covered in blue, yellow etc. But anyway, now the excitement is passed and no harm's done, the worst of it was that I lost my painting which was very soon broken up, along with my easel, bag etc. Impossible to fish anything out. Besides, everything was torn to shreds by the sea, that 'old hag' as your sister calls her. Anyway, I was lucky to escape, but how I raged when I found once I'd changed that I couldn't work, and when it dawned on me that the painting which I had been counting on was done for, I was furious. Immediately I set about telegraphing Troisgros to send me what's missing and an easel will be ready for tomorrow . . .

Letter to Alice Hoschedé, Etretat, November 1885

Storm Coast of Belle-Isle
1886

Musée d'Orsay, Paris

I have nothing finished and you know I can really only judge what I have done when I see it again at home and I always need a moment of peace before giving the final touches to my canvases.

I always work a great deal, I often have bad weather unfortunately, and for many motifs I have diffculty in finding the same effect again, and I will have much to do once I get back to Giverny.

Letter to Durand-Ruel, Belle-Isle, 1886

Creuse Valley, Fresselines
1889

Musée Marmottan, Paris

What a lot of trouble you've had, but at least you're back and it's all over; I, however, am in a state of utter despair and feel like throwing everything into the river; I'm so miserable I didn't feel like writing, but now my mind's made up, you'll cheer me up and it's consoling to talk about one's hardships.

Briefly, yesterday was a very bad day and this morning was worse still; a painting which might have been very good is utterly spoilt and I fear for the others. What's more, the weather's wearing me down, a terrible cold wind which wouldn't have bothered me in the slightest if I'd captured my effect, but the endless succession of clouds and sunny intervals couldn't be worse, especially when I'm getting to the end; but the thing that is upsetting me the most is that with the drought the Creuse is shrinking visibly and its colour is altering so radically that everything around it is transformed. In places where the water once fell in green torrents all you see now is a brown bed. I'm desperate and don't know what to do, as this arid weather is here to stay. None of my paintings are right as they are, and I was counting on these last few days to rescue a good number of them; to give up now would mean that all my efforts have been wasted, but the struggle terrifies me, and I am worn out and longing to come home.

Letter to Alice Hoschedé, Fresselines, April 1889

Grain Stacks, End of Summer
1890-91

Musée d'Orsay, Paris

... I'm hard at it, working stubbornly on the grain stacks, but at this time of the year the sun sets so fast that I can't keep up with it ... I'm getting so slow at my work it makes me despair, but the more I see that a lot of work has to be done in order to render what I'd call 'instantaneity', the 'envelope' above all, the same light spread over everything the more I'm disgusted by easy things that come in one go. Anyway, I'm increasing the need to render what I experience, and I'm praying that I'll have a few good years left to me because I think I may make some progress in that direction ...

Letter to Gustav Geffroy, October 1890

The Poplars, Autumn
1891

Philadelphia Museum of Art
Given by Chester Dale

Whereas you seek philosophically the world in itself, I am simply expending my efforts upon a maximum of appearances, which are in close correlation with unknown realities. When one is dealing with concordant appearances, one cannot be far from reality, or at least what we can know of it. I have done no more than look at what the universe has shown me in order to bear witness to it through my brush. Is that not something? Your mistake is to want to reduce the world to your measure, whereas by enlarging your knowledge of things, you will find your knowledge of self is enlarged.

Reported conversation with Georges Clemenceau at Giverny

Rouen Cathedral, The Portal Front View
1893

Musée d'Orsay, Paris

My stay here is advancing, which doesn't mean that I'm near to finishing my 'Cathedrals'. Regretfully I can only repeat that the further I get, the more difficult it is for me to convey what I feel; and I tell myself that anyone who claims he's finished a painting is terribly arrogant. To finish something means complete, perfect and I'm forcing myself to work, but can't make any progress; looking for something, groping my way forward, but coming up with nothing very special, except to reach the point where I'm exhausted by it all.

Letter to Gustav Geffroy, Rouen, March 1893

What terrible unsettled weather! I carry on regardless without a break. I'm feeling better but, dear God, this cursed cathedral is hard to do! Since I've been here, a week tomorrow, I've worked every day on the same two paintings and can't get what I want; well, it will come in the end, with a hard struggle. I'm very glad I decided to come back, it's better like this . . .

Letter to Alice Monet, March 1893

Rouen Cathedral, Morning
1893

Musée d'Orsay, Paris

I'm working away like a madman but, alas, all your words are in vain, and I feel empty and good for nothing. It all happens at once, the weather isn't very predictable: wonderful sunshine yesterday, fog this morning, sun this afternoon which disappeared just when I needed it; tomorrow it will be a dark grey day or rainy, and once again, I'm very much afraid I'll leave everything and come home on an impulse . . .

What's the good of working when I don't get to the end of anything? This evening I wanted to compare what I've done now with the old paintings, which I don't like looking at too much in case I fall into the same errors. Well, the result of that was that I was right to be unhappy last year; it's ghastly and what I'm doing now is quite as bad, bad in a different way, that's all. The essential thing is to avoid the urge to do it all too quickly, try, try again, and get it right once and for all . . .

Things went a little better today and I'll finish with this cathedral eventually, but it will take time. It's only with hard work that I can achieve what I want; I wouldn't be surprised if once again nothing definitive comes of it, and I might have to come back next year. I'll certainly do all I can to pull through this time; it depends on the weather, but in any case I don't want to prolong work endlessly or alter my paintings as the sun gets higher. Anyway I'm a little happier today, but I'll have deserved my Sunday off . . .

Letters to Alice Monet, Rouen, 1893

Bjornegaard, Norway
1895

Musée Marmottan, Paris

I can see that it's very cold where you are too, but it's nothing compared to here; your night temperatures are our day ones. I can well understand how happy the skaters are, but I dread what's happening to the garden, the bulbs. Is the ice on the pond being watched carefully? It would be very sad if everything planted there were to die. That aside, I now regret that I went away at this time, since apart from my joy in being with Jacques and sending you good news of him, the trip will have served no purpose. Up to now I had thought I'd be able to work. To that end we travelled all day again yesterday and saw more beautiful things, but I can see it will be far too difficult; getting things set up, and the amount of time it takes to go to and fro makes work out of the question. And as I can't see the point of covering canvases only to leave them behind, I'm giving up the idea, much to Jacques' disappointment. All this is making me rather gloomy and I very much regret not being in Giverny, where I might have taken advantage of the fine sights to be seen there at this time of year, and since I've now seen quite enough of Norway, it's quite possible that I'll make my way back to France unannounced, having little desire to see a country which I can't paint.

Letter to Alice Monet, Norway, 1895

Monet's Garden at Giverny
1900

Musée d'Orsay, Paris

Sowing: around 300 pots Poppies – 60 Sweet pea – around 60 pots white Agremony – 30 yellow Agremony – Blue sage – Blue Waterlilies in beds greenhouse – Dahlias – Iris Kaempferi. – From the 15th to the 25th, lay the dahlias down to root; plant out those with shoots before I get back. – Don't forget the lily bulbs. – Should the Japanese paeonies arrive plant them immediately if weather permits, taking care initially to protect buds from the cold, as much as from the heat of the sun. Get down to pruning: rose trees not too long, except for the thorny varieties. In March sow the grass seeds, plant out the little nasturtiums, keep a close eye on the gloxinia, orchids etc, in the greenhouse, as well as the plants under frames. Trim the borders as arranged; put wires in for the clematis and climbing roses as soon as Picard has done the necessary. If the weather's bad, make some straw matting, but lighter than previously. Plant cuttings from the rose trees at the pond around manure in the hen huts. Don't delay work on tarring the planks and plant the Helianthus cariflorus in good clumps right away. If anything's missing such as manure, pots etc, ask Madame if possible on a Friday so as to have it on Saturday. In March force the chrysanthemums along as the buds won't open in damp conditions; and don't forget to put the sulphur sheets back over the greenhouse frames.

Monet's notes to his gardener, Giverny, 1900

Houses of Parliament
1904

Musée d'Orsay, Paris

... But what weather and how gloomy I was at the prospect of being unable to paint! Fortunately I had a better day than expected, I was able to work before and after lunch from my window and at 5, with the sun setting gloriously in the mist, I started work at the hospital. If only you could have seen how beautiful it was and how I wished you were here on the terrace with me; it seems it was cold and I was oblivious to it in my enthusiasm for the work in hand and for the novelty of it all, but how hard it's going to be!

Letter to Alice Monet, London, 1904

Water-Lilies
1907

Musée Marmottan, Paris

Like you I'm sorry not to be able to exhibit the 'Water-lilies' series this year, and if I made this decision it's because it was impossible. Perhaps it's true that I'm very hard on myself, but that's better than exhibiting mediocre work. And I'm not delaying the exhibition because I'm keen to show a lot of work, far from it, but too few were satisfactory enough to trouble the public with. At the very most I have five or six that are possible; moreover I've just destroyed thirty at least and this entirely to my satisfaction.

I still have a lot of pleasure doing them, but as time goes by I come to appreciate more clearly which paintings are good and which should be discarded. All the same, this doesn't affect my eagerness and confidence that I can do better.

Letter to Gustav Geffroy, Giverny, 1907

... You must know I'm entirely absorbed in my work. These landscapes of water and reflections have become an obsession. It's quite beyond my powers at my age, and yet I want to succeed in expressing what I feel. I've destroyed some ... I start others ... and I hope that something will come out of so much effort ...

Letter to Durand-Ruel, Giverny, 1907

[67]

View of San Giorgio Maggiore, Venice
1908

The National Museum of Wales

Absorbed as I was in my work, I was unable to write to you and so I handed my wife the task of giving you the news. She no doubt told you of my enthusiasm for Venice. Well, it increases by the day and I'm very sad that I'll soon have to leave this unique light. It's so very beautiful, but we must resign ourselves to the inevitable; I have many pressing obligations at home. I comfort myself wth the thought that I'll come back next year, since I've only made some studies, some beginnings. But what a shame I didn't come here when I was a younger man, when I was full of daring! Still ... I've spent some thoughtful hours here, almost forgetting that I'm now an old man ...

Best wishes from my wife and myself.

Letter to Durand-Ruel, Venice, 1908

Venice, the Ducal Palace
1908-1912

Brooklyn Museum, New York

I am overcome with admiration for Venice, but unfortunately I can't stay here long so there's no hope of doing any serious work. I am doing a few paintings in any case, to have a record of the place, but I intend to spend a whole season here next year. I don't yet know when we'll be back. It will depend on the weather.

Letter to Durand-Ruel, Venice, 1908

Water-Lily Decorations, Morning with Willows
1916-26

Musée de l'Orangerie, Paris

I'm making the best of the bad weather today to let you know how I am and also ask you whether, as I hope, you'll stop here on your return journey, in which case I'd like some idea of when you're coming as I'm planning a couple of short breaks and wouldn't like to miss you.

I've been working hard and non-stop during this marvellous weather. I wouldn't presume to say I was satisfied with what I've done, although I believe I've made some progress. My health is better and I wish next year was here already so that I could carry on my research in spite of my poor eyesight.

Letter to Bernheim-Jeune, Giverny, 1921

Sunset on the Seine, Winter
1880

Musée du Petit Palais, Paris

I would have replied myself to the requests you directed to Madame Jean Monet, but for some while I've been in a state of utter despair and I'm disgusted with all I've done. Day by day my sight is going and I can sense only too well that with it comes an end to my long-cherished hopes to do better. It's very sad to have come to this; all this to say that I see little point in answering your questions. My work belongs to the public, and people can say what they like about it; I've done what I could.

Letter to Froy, Giverny, January 1920

Self Portrait
1910

Collection Durand-Ruel, Paris

... I'm in a very black mood and am profoundly disgusted with painting. It really is a continual torture! Don't expect to see anything new, the little I did manage to do has been destroyed, scraped off or torn up. You've no idea what appalling weather we've had continuously these past two months. When you're trying to convey the weather, the atmosphere and the general mood, it's enough to make you mad with rage.

On top of all this, I've stupidly succumbed to rheumatism. I'm paying for my sessions in rain and snow and it's distressing to think that I'll have to stop braving all weathers and not work outside except when it's fine. What a stupid business life is! ...

Letter to Gustav Geffroy, Giverny, July 1890

CHRONOLOGY

Claude Oscar Monet
1840-1926

1840   Born in Paris on 14 November, the elder son of a grocer.

1845   The family move to Le Havre, where Monet grows up.

1857   Makes friends with Boudin who introduces him to landscape painting *en plein air*.

1859   Meets Pissarro at the Académie Suisse in Paris.

1861   In Algeria for military service.

1862   Meets Renoir, Sisley and Bazille at Charles Gleyre's studio.

1865   Paints 'Déjeuner sur l'Herbe'.
        Exhibits at Paris Salon.

1870   Marries Camille Doncieux, mother of his son, Jean. They honeymoon at Trouville.
        Goes to London with Pissarro to escape the Franco-Prussian War.

1871   Impressionism formed at this period in Argenteuil, where Monet paints from a houseboat and is visited by Manet, Renoir and Sisley.

1878   Moves to Vétheuil with his family, and Alice Hoschedé and her children.

1879   Camille dies of consumption.

1880   Starts annual trips to the coast at Normandy.

1883   Moves to Giverny where he buys a house in 1890, living
there for the rest of his life.

1884   Visits Bordighera.

1886   Visits Belle-Isle.

1888   Visits Antibes.

1889   Visits Creuse Valley.

1891   Begins to paint series of Poplars and Haystacks.

1892   Marries Alice Hoschedé following the death of her
husband.

1893   Builds water garden with water-lilies at Giverny.

1893   Begins painting Rouen Cathedral.

1895   Visits Norway.

1897   Goes on painting trip to Pourville.

1904   London paintings exhibited.

1911   Alice Monet dies.
Monet beginning to suffer increasingly from the effects of
cataract, which is finally operated on in 1923.

1916   Commissioned by Clemenceau to paint Water-Lily decorations.

1922   Water-Lily decorations presented to the State to be exhibited
at the Orangerie.

1926   Dies at Giverny on 6 December, aged eighty-six.

ACKNOWLEDGEMENTS

The editor and publishers would like to thank the following for their help in providing the photographs of paintings reproduced in this book:

Art Institute of Chicago (p43)
Bridgeman Art Library (p69)
Brooklyn Museum, New York (p71)
Cleveland Museum of Art (p39)
Detroit Institute of Arts (p13)
Durand-Ruel & CIE, Paris (pp7, 16, 77)
Fogg Art Museum, Harvard University, Cambridge, Mass (p45)
Kimbell Art Museum, Fort Worth, Texas (p21: photo Michael Bodycomb)
Kunsthalle, Bremen (p23)
Kunsthaus, Zurich, VZK (p41)
Museum of Fine Arts, Boston (frontispiece, p14)
National Gallery, London (pp25, 29, 33)
National Gallery of Art, Washington DC (cover, pp9, 37)
National Museum of Wales, Cardiff (p63)
Philadelphia Museum of Art (pp15, 53)
Photo RMN (pp27, 31, 35, 47, 51, 55, 57, 61, 65, 73)
Photographie Giraudon (p75)
Private Collection (p19)
Studio Lourmel 77 (pp12, 49, 59, 67)
Toledo Museum of Art (p10)

We would also like to thank the publishers of the following books for access to the material contained in them which has been reproduced in this volume:

Monet, Biography and Catalogue Raisonné Daniel Wildenstein 1985
Renoir, My Father Jean Renoir 1962

Every effort has been made to contact the owners of the copyright of all the information contained in this book, but if, for any reason, any acknowledgements have been omitted, the publishers ask those concerned to contact them.